Charles Causley

SELECTED POEMS
FOR CHILDREN

Illustrated by John Lawrence

MACMILLAN
CHILDREN'S BOOKS

First published 1997 by Macmillan Children's Books
a division of Macmillan Publishers Limited
25 Eccleston Place, London SW1W 9NF
and Basingstoke
www.macmillan.co.uk

Associated companies throughout the world

ISBN 0 330 35404 3

Text copyright © Charles Causley 1997
Illustrations © John Lawrence 1997

The right of Charles Causley and John Lawrence to be identified as the
author and illustrator of this work has been asserted by them in accordance
with the Copyright, Designs and Patents Act 1988.

7 9 8 6

A CIP catalogue record for this book is available from
the British Library.

Phototypeset by Intype London Ltd
Printed and bound in Great Britain by
Mackays of Chatham plc, Kent

SELECTED POEMS
FOR CHILDREN

CHARLES CAUSLEY lives in his native town of Launceston in Cornwall, with his beloved ginger cat, Rupert. Apart from six years in the Royal Navy, Causley has spent almost all his life in Launceston, where he also once worked as a teacher. He has published many collections of his work for both adults and children. He has been the recipient of a number of literary awards and prizes, including the Kurt Maschler Award, the Signal Poetry Award and (from the USA) the Ingersoll/T.S. Eliot Award. He is a Fellow of the Royal Society of Literature and has received the Queen's Gold Medal for Poetry. In 1986 Charles Causley was appointed CBE.

JOHN LAWRENCE lives in Cambridge and has illustrated over a hundred books including *Watership Down* by Richard Adams and *Robin Hood* for Macmillan. He has twice been the winner of the Francis Williams Illustration Awards, is a Fellow of the Royal Society of Printmakers and the Society of Wood Engravers and was Master of the Art Workers' Guild in 1990. To illustrate these poems, John Lawrence travelled to Cornwall, to meet Charles Causley and to make sure the drawings were accurate, since so many of the poems refer to real places in and around Launceston. If you look carefully, you will find many references to Cornwall, its history and traditions throughout the book.

To
Lorna, Paul
and
Alistair White

Contents

GIVE ME A HOUSE

Give me a house, said Polly.
Give me land, said Hugh.
Give me the moon, said Sadie.
Give me the sun, said Sue.

Give me a horse, said Rollo.
Give me a hound, said Joe.
Give me fine linen, said Sarah.
Give me silk, said Flo.

Give me a mountain, said Kirsty.
Give me a valley, said Jim.
Give me a river, said Dodo.
Give me the sky, said Tim.

Give me the ocean, said Adam.
Give me a ship, said Hal.
Give me a kingdom, said Rory.
Give me a crown, said Sal.

Give me gold, said Peter.
Give me silver, said Paul.
Give me love, said Jenny,
Or nothing at all.

KING FOO FOO

King Foo Foo sat upon his throne
Dressed in his royal closes,
While all around his courtiers stood
With clothes-pegs on their noses.

'This action strange,' King Foo Foo said,
'My mind quite discomposes,
Though vulgar curiosity
A good king never shoses.'

But to the court it was as clear
As poetry or prose is:
King Foo Foo had not had a bath
Since goodness only knoses.

Till one fine day the Fire Brigade
Rehearsing with their hoses
(To Handel's 'Water Music' played
With many puffs and bloses)

Quite failed the water to control
In all its ebbs and floses
And simply drenched the King with sev-
Eral thousand gallon doses.

At this each wight (though impolite)
A mighty grin exposes.
'At last,' the King said, 'now I see
That all my court morose is!

'A debt to keep his courtiers glad
A monarch surely oweses,
And deep within my royal breast
A sporting heart reposes.'

So now each night its water bright
The Fire Brigade disposes
Over a King who smiles as sweet
As all the royal roses.

THE YOUNG MAN OF CURY

I am the Young Man of Cury,
I lie on the lip of the sand,
I comb the blown sea with five fingers
To call my true-love to the land.

She gave me a comb made of coral,
She told me to comb the green tide
And she would rise out of the ocean
To lie on the strand by my side.

Her hair flowed about her like water,
Her gaze it was blue, it was bold,
And half of her body was silver
And half of her body was gold.

One day as I lay by the flood-tide
And drew the bright comb to and fro
The sea snatched it out of my fingers
And buried it in the dark flow.

She promised me that she would teach me
All the hours of waking, of sleep,
The mysteries of her salt country,
The runes and the tunes of the deep;

How spells may be broken, how sickness
Be cured with a word I might tell,
The thief be discovered, the future
Be plain as these pebbles, this shell.

My son and his son and his also,
She said, would be heir to such charm
And their lives and their loves hold in safety
For ever from evil and harm.

But never a song does she sing me,
Nor ever a word does she say
Since I carried her safe where the tide-mark
Is scored on the sands of the bay.

I am the Young Man of Cury,
I lie on the lip of the sand,
I comb the blown sea with five fingers
To call my true-love to the land.

Cury is a village near Lizard Point in Cornwall. Cornish legends tell of how a
fisherman from Cury rescued a stranded mermaid and returned her to the sea.
Robert Hunt has a version called 'The Old Man of Cury' in his *Popular
Romances of the West of England* (1881), set in Kynance Cove, also in the
Lizard Peninsula.

Mary, Mary Magdalene

Mary, Mary Magdalene
Lying on the wall,
I throw a pebble on your back.
Will it lie or fall?

Send me down for Christmas
Some stockings and some hose,
And send before the winter's end
A brand-new suit of clothes.

Mary, Mary Magdalene
Under a stony tree,
I throw a pebble on your back.
What will you send me?

I'll send you for your Christening
A woollen robe to wear,
A shiny cup from which to sup,
And a name to bear.

Mary, Mary Magdalene
Lying cool as snow,
What will you be sending me
When to school I go?

I'll send a pencil and a pen
That write both clean and neat.
And I'll send to the schoolmaster
A tongue that's kind and sweet.

Mary, Mary Magdalene
Lying in the sun,
What will you be sending me
Now I'm twenty-one?

I'll send you down a locket
As silver as your skin,
And I'll send you a lover
To fit a gold key in.

Mary, Mary Magdalene
Underneath the spray,
What will you be sending me
On my wedding-day?

I'll send you down some blossom,
Some ribbons and some lace,
And for the bride a veil to hide
The blushes on her face.

Mary, Mary Magdalene
Whiter than the swan,
Tell me what you'll send me,
Now my good man's dead and gone.

> *I'll send to you a single bed*
> *On which you must lie,*
> *And pillows bright where tears may light*
> *That fall from your eye.*

Mary, Mary Magdalene
Now nine months are done,
What will you be sending me
For my little son?

> *I'll send you for your baby*
> *A lucky stone, and small,*
> *To throw to Mary Magdalene*
> *Lying on the wall.*

On the south wall of the church of St Mary Magdalene at Launceston in Cornwall is a granite figure of the saint. The children of the town say that a stone lodged on her back will bring good luck.

HAZEL

Hazel fork
From hazel tree
Tell me where
The waters be.

Hazel shoot
In my hand
Bring me where
My true-love stands.

Hazel stem,
Hazel leaf,
Show me robber,
Show me thief.

Hazel twig,
Hazel bud,
Keep my house
From fire and flood.

Hazel stick,
Hazel wand,
Save me from
A salt-sea end.

Hazel bush,
Hazel tree,
May you ever
Dwell by me.

'QUACK!' SAID THE BILLY-GOAT

'Quack!' said the billy-goat.
  'Oink!' said the hen.
'Miaow!' said the little chick
  Running in the pen.

'Hobble-gobble!' said the dog.
  'Cluck!' said the sow.
'Tu-whit tu-whoo!' the donkey said.
  'Baa!' said the cow.

'Hee-haw!' the turkey cried.
  The duck began to moo.
All at once the sheep went,
  'Cock-a-doodle-doo!'

The owl coughed and cleared his throat
  And he began to bleat.
'Bow-wow!' said the cock
  Swimming in the leat.

'Cheep-cheep!' said the cat
  As she began to fly.
'Farmer's been and laid an egg –
  That's the reason why.'

OUT IN THE DESERT

Out in the desert lies the sphinx
It never eats and it never drinx
Its body quite solid without any chinx
And when the sky's all purples and pinx
(As if it was painted with coloured inx)
And the sun it ever so swiftly sinx
Behind the hills in a couple of twinx
You may hear (if you're lucky) a bell that clinx
And also tolls and also tinx
And they say at the very same sound the sphinx
It sometimes smiles and it sometimes winx:

But nobody knows just what it thinx.

TELL ME, TELL ME, SARAH JANE

Tell me, tell me, Sarah Jane,
   Tell me, dearest daughter,
Why are you holding in your hand
   A thimbleful of water?
Why do you hold it to your eye
   And gaze both late and soon
From early morning light until
   The rising of the moon?

Mother, I hear the mermaids cry,
   I hear the mermen sing,
And I can see the sailing-ships
   All made of sticks and string.
And I can see the jumping fish,
   The whales that fall and rise
And swim about the waterspout
   That swarms up to the skies.

Tell me, tell me, Sarah Jane,
   Tell your darling mother,
Why do you walk beside the tide
   As though you loved none other?
Why do you listen to a shell
   And watch the billows curl,
And throw away your diamond ring
   And wear instead the pearl?

Mother, I hear the water
  Beneath the headland pinned,
And I can see the sea-gull
  Sliding down the wind.
I taste the salt upon my tongue
  As sweet as sweet can be.

Tell me, my dear, whose voice you hear?

It is the sea, the sea.

JEREMY PEEP

Jeremy Peep
When fast asleep
Walks the level
And walks the steep
Eyes tight shut
And face quite pale
His night-shirt billowing
Like a sail.
Down the stairway
And up the street
With nothing at all
Upon his feet.
His arms out straight
In front of his face
He zigs and zags
All over the place.
He never stumbles,
He never slips,
It's as if he could see
With his finger-tips.
'Don't make him open
As much as an eye,'
The neighbours ever so
Softly sigh,
'Or out of his noddle
His wits will fly!
Just turn him about
And watch him head
Straight back home
To his truckle-bed
And sure and slow

He'll get back in
And draw the covers
Up to his chin.'
And the neighbours they tut
About this and that
And say, 'Jeremy, Jeremy,
What were you at
When the moon was up
And the stars were few
And the Town Hall clock
Was striking two?
Have you *any* idea
Where you were last night
When most good people
Were tucked up tight?'
'Such questions you ask!'
Says Jeremy Peep.
'So silly they strike me
All of a heap!
Walking the town
So wild and wan
With nothing at all
But my night-shirt on?
I can't understand
Why you think I should keep
Such curious habits,'
Says Jeremy Peep.
'Where was I all last night?

Asleep.'

DIGGORY PRANCE

Diggory Prance, Diggory Prance
Paid his bills with a bit of a dance.

He took a whistle, he took a drum,
He'd trip it and skip it till kingdom come.

He danced for the butcher who brought him meat
The whole of the length of Shambles Street.

He danced for the baker who baked his bread.
He danced for the tailor, his needle and thread.

He danced for his rent, he danced for his rates.
He danced for the builder who fixed his slates.

He danced for the cobbler who mended his shoe,
He danced for the plumber, the painter too.

He danced for his light, he danced for his heat.
He danced for his takeaway, sour-and-sweet.

He danced for the dentist, the doctor, the draper.
He danced for the price of his daily paper –

Till came a day when, 'Now, dear Diggory, please,
It's time,' said the Mayor, 'for this nonsense to cease.

'You must settle in cash and in coin what you owe
Or I fear I must ask you to pack up and go.'

But all of the people cried, 'What? What? What?
    What?
Send away Diggory? Certainly not!

'Send away Diggory? Never a chance!
We *like* to see Diggory doing a dance!

'We trust we are making it perfectly plain –
So please never mention the subject again.

'Never, whatever the wind or the weather,
Please never mention the subject again

'Of Diggory Prance, Diggory Prance
Who pays his bills with a bit of a dance.'

TOMORROW IS SIMNEL SUNDAY

Tomorrow is Simnel Sunday
And homeward I shall steer
And I must bake a simnel cake
For my mother dear.

I'll fetch me almonds, cherries,
The finest in the land,
I'll fetch me salt, I'll fetch me spice,
I'll fetch me marzipan.

With milk and eggs and butter
And flour as fair as snow
And raisins sweet and candied treat
I'll set it all to go.

And I shall search for violets
That scent the homeward way
For tomorrow is Simnel Sunday
And it is Mothering Day.

Simnel (or Mothering) Sunday is the fourth Sunday in Lent. Following an old custom, children visited their parents for the day and took gifts of cake and flowers.

When I Was a Hundred and Twenty-six

When I was a hundred and twenty-six
And you were a hundred and four
What fun, my dearest dear, we had
At the back of the Co-op store.
It was all such a very long time ago
That it seems just like a dream
In the days when you called me your own Rich Tea
And you were my Custard Cream.

Such joys we knew with those dinners *à deux*
At the bottom of the parking lot
On roasted gnu and buffalo stew
And Tandoori chicken in a pot.
Such songs, my love, we used to sing
Till the stars had lost their shine,
And the bells of heaven rang ding, ding, ding
And the neighbours rang 999.

When I was a hundred and twenty-six
And you were a hundred and four
We thought love's cherry would last a very
Long time, and then some more.
But days are fleet when ways are sweet
As the honey in a hive –
And I am a hundred and twenty-seven
And you are a hundred and five.

FABLE

I was a slave on Samos, a small man
Carelessly put together; face a mask
So frightful that at first the people ran
Away from me, especially at dusk.

I was possessed, too, of a rattling tongue
That only now and then would let words pass
As they should properly be said or sung.
In general, you could say I was a mess.

One thing redeemed me. People marvelled at
The brilliance with which my speech was woven.
It was, they said, as if a toad had spat
Diamonds. And my ugliness was forgiven.

Soon I was freed, and sooner was the friend
Of kings and commoners who came a-calling.
Of my bright hoard of wit there seemed no end,
Nor of the tales that I rejoiced in telling.

But there were heads and hearts where, green and
    cold,
The seeds of envy and of hate were lying.
From our most sacred shrine, a cup of gold
Was hidden in my store, myself unknowing.

'Sacrilege! He is thief!' my accusers swore,
And to the cliffs of Delphi I was taken,
Hurled to the myrtle-scented valley floor
And on its whitest stones my body broken.

'This is the end of him and his poor fame!'
I heard them cry upon the gleaming air.
Stranger, now tell me if you know my name,
My story of the Tortoise and the Hare?

Perhaps it's appropriate that the most famous writer of fables, known to us as
Aesop, also has what are probably a great many unhistorical and legendary
stories told about his life. The poem collects some of these 'facts' together:
including the belief that he had a stammer. If Aesop was one person (and not,
as some scholars say, merely the name given to a whole group of story-tellers)
it is at least fairly certain that he lived in about the sixth century BC.

TIMOTHY WINTERS

Timothy Winters comes to school
With eyes as wide as a football pool,
Ears like bombs and teeth like splinters:
A blitz of a boy is Timothy Winters.

His belly is white, his neck is dark,
And his hair is an exclamation mark.
His clothes are enough to scare a crow
And through his britches the blue winds blow.

When teacher talks he won't hear a word
And he shoots down dead the arithmetic-bird,
He licks the patterns off his plate
And he's not even heard of the Welfare State.

Timothy Winters has bloody feet
And he lives in a house on Suez Street,
He sleeps in a sack on the kitchen floor
And they say there aren't boys like him any more.

Old Man Winters likes his beer
And his missus ran off with a bombardier,
Grandma sits in the grate with a gin
And Timothy's dosed with an aspirin.

The Welfare Worker lies awake
But the law's as tricky as a ten-foot snake,
So Timothy Winters drinks his cup
And slowly goes on growing up.

At Morning Prayers the Master helves[1]
For children less fortunate than ourselves,
And the loudest response in the room is when
Timothy Winters roars 'Amen!'

So come one angel, come on ten:
Timothy Winters says 'Amen
Amen amen amen amen.'
Timothy Winters, Lord.

                             Amen.

[1] *helves*: a dialect word from north Cornwall used to describe the alarmed lowing of cattle (as when a cow is separated from her calf); a desperate, pleading note.

MILLER'S END

When we moved to Miller's End,
   Every afternoon at four
A thin shadow of a shade
   Quavered through the garden-door.

Dressed in black from top to toe
   And a veil about her head
To us all it seemed as though
   She came walking from the dead.

With a basket on her arm
   Through the hedge-gap she would pass,
Never a mark that we could spy
   On the flagstones or the grass.

When we told the garden-boy
   How we saw the phantom glide,
With a grin his face was bright
   As the pool he stood beside.

'That's no ghost-walk,' Billy said.
  'Nor a ghost you fear to stop –
Only old Miss Wickerby
  On a short cut to the shop.'

So next day we lay in wait,
  Passed a civil time of day,
Said how pleased we were she came
  Daily down our garden-way.

Suddenly her cheek it paled,
  Turned, as quick, from ice to flame.
'Tell me,' said Miss Wickerby.
  'Who spoke of me, and my name?'

'Bill the garden-boy.'
                  She sighed,
  Said, 'Of course, you could not know
How he drowned – that very pool –
  A frozen winter – long ago.'

As I Went Down Zig Zag

As I went down Zig Zag
  The clock striking one,
I saw a man cooking
  An egg in the sun.

        As I went down Zig Zag
          The clock striking two,
        I watched a man walk
          With one boot and one shoe.

As I went down Zig Zag
  The clock striking three,
I heard a man murmuring
  'Buzz!' like a bee.

        As I went down Zig Zag
          The clock striking four,
        I saw a man swim
          In no sea by no shore.

As I went down Zig Zag
  The clock striking five,
I caught a man keeping
  A hog in a hive.

As I went down Zig Zag
The clock striking six,
I met a man making
A blanket of bricks.

As I went down Zig Zag
The clock striking seven,
A man asked me if
I was odd or was even.

As I went down Zig Zag
The clock striking eight,
I saw a man sailing
A seven-barred gate.

As I went down Zig Zag
The clock striking nine,
I saw a man milking
Where never were kine.

As I went down Zig Zag
  The clock striking ten,
I watched a man waltz
  With a cock and a hen.

As I went down Zig Zag
  The clock striking eleven,
I saw a man baking
  A loaf with no leaven.

As I went down Zig Zag
  The clock striking twelve,
For dyes from the rainbow
  I saw a man delve.

So if you'd keep your senses,
  The point of my rhyme
Is don't go down Zig Zag
  When the clocks start to chime.

Zig Zag is the name of a steep footpath in Launceston.

TOM BONE

My name is Tom Bone,
I live all alone
In a deep house on Winter Street.
  Through my mud wall
  The wolf-spiders crawl
  And the mole has his beat.

On my roof of green grass
All the day footsteps pass
In the heat and the cold,
  As snug in a bed
  With my name at its head
  One great secret I hold.

Tom Bone, when the owls rise
In the drifting night skies
Do you walk round about?
  All the solemn hours through
  I lie down just like you
  And sleep the night out.

Tom Bone, as you lie there
On your pillow of hair,
What grave thoughts do you keep?
  Tom says, Nonsense and stuff!
  You'll know soon enough.
  Sleep, darling, sleep.

PRINCE IVO

Prince Ivo by the castle stood
He built with his own hand.
He looked towards the wandering sea,
He looked towards the land.

Tall was the yellow tower where
Prince Ivo's flag was flown.
The moat was wide, the moat was deep,
The gate was all of stone.

'And none there is,' Prince Ivo said,
'Shall bring my castle low,
For I am Lord of all I see
Wherever I may go.'

But there was one that heard him speak
And by his castle lay
Crept up the evening strand and washed
His house of sand away.

And when at sunfall Ivo came
Down to the silent shore
There was no sign of wall or tower.
His castle was no more.

Never a sign did Ivo show
Of sorrow or of pain,
But took his sturdy spade in hand
To build his house again.

Prince Ivo smiled and shook his head.
Softly I heard him say,
'Tomorrow, but tomorrow
Is another day.'

THE ELEPHANT AND THE BUTTERFLY

Said the elephant to the butterfly
As they wandered the forest through,
'I wish I could rise up into the skies
And flutter about like you!
If I was as fine as a feather
I'd ramble the wide air round.
It's a terrible bore to never get more
Than a couple of feet off the ground!'

Said the butterfly to the elephant,
'My dear, that sounds perfectly fine.
You could make yourself wings out of palms and
    things
With the aid of the creeper and vine.
If you turn your trunk like a propeller
In a bit of a following breeze
There's no reason why you won't take to the sky
With simply incredible ease.'

Believe it or not, but no sooner
Had the butterfly uttered these words
Than the elephant flew straight up in the blue
As though he was one of the birds.
High over the trees of the jungle
And high above mountain and scree
The elephant wobbled and wavered
Over land and then over the sea.

'Good gracious!' he cried, and, 'Good heavens!
I'm dizzy from toe to my crown,
And my memory's bad (and isn't it sad?)
But when things go up they come down.
My head it is rolling and reeling
And my stomach has gone on the spree.
I've a notion that if I don't land in the ocean
It's curtains for certain for me!'

But the lucky old elephant landed
In the softest of sea and of sand
And he paddled ashore with a bit of a roar
And sat himself down on the land.
He lifted his voice to the hill-tops
With an elephant trumpet-y sound.
'Do you think, butterfly, I was foolish to try?'
But the creature was nowhere around.

And ever since then you will find him
(That is, if you're anxious to look)
Reclining and reading an encyclopaedian
Sort of a Reference Book.
He studies it morning and evening
(Now and then gazing up in the sky)
On 'How Best to Sight the Butterfly (White)'

And a faraway look in his eye.

MRS COLÓN

Mrs Colón,
Christopher's gone
Sailing a boat
On the herring pond.

Says he's sure
That he knows best,
Steering, speering
West and west.

We gave him a call,
We gave him a shout
But he simply refuses
To turn about.

Will he remember
To keep in his head
The sooth of what
The schoolmaster said,

That the world is flat
With never a bend,
Go too far
And you're off the end

Mrs Colón,
What's to be done?
Christopher's sailing
The herring pond.

In English-speaking countries the Italian sailor Cristoforo Colombo (or, in Spain, Cristobal Colón) is known as Christopher Columbus.

ALL DAY SATURDAY

Let it sleet on Sunday,
Monday let it snow,
Let the mist on Tuesday
From the salt-sea flow.
Let it hail on Wednesday,
Thursday let it rain,
Let the wind on Friday
Blow a hurricane,
But Saturday, Saturday
Break fair and fine
And all day Saturday
Let the sun shine.

TOMMY HYDE

Tommy Hyde, Tommy Hyde,
What are you doing by the salt-sea side?

Picking up pebbles and smoothing sand
And writing a letter on the ocean strand.

Tommy Hyde, Tommy Hyde,
Why do you wait by the turning tide?

I'm watching for the water to rub it off the shore
And take it to my true-love in Baltimore.

A Mermaid at Zennor

A mermaid at Zennor
Climbed out of the sea
By the seething Zennor shore.
Her gown was silver,
Her gown was gold
And a crown of pearl she wore,
She wore,
A crown of pearl she wore.

The Zennor bay
Burned peacock-blue,
White was the Zennor sand
Where she came up
By Zennor Head,
Comb in her crystal hand,
Her hand,
Comb in her crystal hand.

She stood before
The great church door
That open was and wide.
She gazed into
The mirror true
She carried at her side,
Her side,
She carried at her side.

Now Zennor men
Do love to sing
Their songs both great and small,
And Sampson Scown
The Squire's son
Sang sweetest of them all,
Them all,
Sang sweetest of them all.

The mermaid stepped
Out of the sun
And slowly entered in,
Her purpose fell
By charm or spell
Young Sampson for to win,
To win,
Young Sampson for to win.

And in a sea-deep
Tongue she sang
A song that none
Had known,
And choir and congregation stood
As they were made of stone,
Of stone,
As they were made of stone.

Only Young Sampson
Made reply
As clear as Cornish gold,
For he and only he
Could tell
The salt song that she told,
She told,
The salt song that she told.

She beckoned where
Young Sampson stood.
He took her by the hand.
And one and one
They walked them down
Towards the Zennor strand,
The strand,
Towards the Zennor strand.

And did they ever
Come again
There's never a one
Will own,
Where still in church
The people stand
As they were made of stone,
Of stone,
As they were made of stone.

Zennor is on the coast of the far west of Cornwall, and is a village once renowned for its singers. The church, dedicated to the Virgin St Sinara or Sener, has a fifteenth-century bench-end bearing a splendid carving of its famous mermaid, complete with comb and glass.

Morwenstow

Where do you come from, sea,
To the sharp Cornish shore,
Leaping up to the raven's crag?
    From Labrador.

Do you grow tired, sea?
Are you weary ever
When the storms burst over your head?
    Never.

Are you hard as a diamond, sea,
As iron, as oak?
Are you stronger than flint or steel?
    And the lightning stroke.

Ten thousand years and more, sea,
You have gobbled your fill,
Swallowing stone and slate!
    I am hungry still.

When will you rest, sea?
    When moon and sun
    Ride only fields of salt water
    And the land is gone.

AT NINE OF THE NIGHT I OPENED MY DOOR

At nine of the night I opened my door
That stands midway between moor and moor,
And all around me, silver-bright,
I saw that the world had turned to white.

Thick was the snow on field and hedge
And vanished was the river-sedge,
Where winter skilfully had wound
A shining scarf without a sound.

And as I stood and gazed my fill
A stable-boy came down the hill.
With every step I saw him take
Flew at his heel a puff of flake.

His brow was whiter than the hoar,
A beard of freshest snow he wore,
And round about him, snowflake starred,
A red horse-blanket from the yard.

In a red cloak I saw him go,
His back was bent, his step was slow,
And as he laboured through the cold
He seemed a hundred winters old.

I stood and watched the snowy head,
The whiskers white, the cloak of red.
'A Merry Christmas!' I heard him cry.
'The same to you, old friend,' said I.

WHO?

Who is that child I see wandering, wandering
Down by the side of the quivering stream?
Why does he seem not to hear, though I call to him?
Where does he come from, and what is his name?

Why do I see him at sunrise and sunset
Taking, in old-fashioned clothes, the same track?
Why, when he walks, does he cast not a shadow
Though the sun rises and falls at his back?

Why does the dust lie so thick on the hedgerow
By the great field where a horse pulls the plough?
Why do I see only meadows, where houses
Stand in a line by the riverside now?

Why does he move like a wraith by the water,
Soft as the thistledown on the breeze blown?
When I draw near him so that I may hear him,
Why does he say that his name is my own?

THREE GREEN SAILORS

Three green sailors
Went to sea
In a sailing ship
Called *The Flying Flea*.
Their caps were round,
Their shirts were square,
Their trousers were rolled
And their feet were bare.
One wore a pigtail,
One wore a patch,
One wore ear-rings
That never did match.
One chewed baccy,
One chewed cake,
One chewed a pennyworth
Of two-eyed steak.[1]
One danced to,
One danced fro
And the other sang the shanty
Haul Away Joe.

They cried 'Belay!'
They called 'Avast!'
They hoisted the sail
To the top of the mast.
They cast off aft,
They cast off fore
And away they sailed
From the steady shore.
'There's never a doubt,'
Said the sailors three,
'That *this* is the life
For the likes of we!'

But soon it was clear
As clear could be
Three green sailors
Were all at sea:
For nothing they knew
Of· star or sun
And nothing of nav-i-
Ga-ti-on,
And they'd no idea
(For they'd never been taught)
Which was starboard
And which was port.
They never did compass
Nor chart possess
Nor a lamp nor a rocket
For an SOS.
But three green sailors
Thought it a ball
And weren't in the least
Bit troubled at all.

The sea rose up,
The light grew thin
And the tide it turned them
Out and in.
The winds blew high
As about they spun
And the thunder sounded
Like a gun.
The Flying Flea
Through the waves it flew
And sometimes *under*
The water too.
In ocean salt,
In ocean cold,
The Flying Flea
It rocked and rolled.

It shook from stem
To stern until
Three green sailors
Were greener still.
'Dear us!' they cried
And 'Help!' they roared
As the wind it whined
And the water poured.
'It's a shock,' they said,
'To our systems three
How quickly the weather
May change at sea.
Not a minute ago
The sky looked great
And now we're in the middle
Of a gale (force 8).
And another fact
We just can't skip:
We don't know a THING
About seamanship.'
So they wept, they cried
And they went all numb
And they felt their very
Last hour had come.

But old King Neptune
Down below
Heard them sobbing
Like billy-o.
He smiled a smile,
He winked an eye
And he said, 'I'll give them
One more try,
For sure as a pound
Is a hundred pence
Another time
They'll show more sense
And I've led those lubbers
Such a dance
I think they deserve
Another chance.
But before again
They take to the sea
They really must learn
A thing or three,
For those who sail
The mighty blue
Should be skilled as seamen
Through and through.
They must learn the trade
From a to zee
Or they'll all end up
Down here with me.'

And now with a blow
Of his salt-sea hand
He washed the good ship
Back to land
And three green sailors
Came ashore
Wiser by far
Than they were before.
'O never,' they said,
'Will we sail the brine
In weather that's foul
Or weather that's fine
Till we learn as well
As well can be
The ways of a sailor,
A ship and the sea.'

And with knees of jelly
And a wavery tread
Each went home
To his own sweet bed.
And Neptune laughed
On the ocean floor
And he stirred the waters
Just once more.
He stirred the waters,
He sang a salt rhyme
And he stirred the waters
One more time,
For he never will tire,
He never will sleep:
Neptune, Neptune,
King of the Deep.

¹ 'Two-eyed steak' is sailors' slang for a bloater or a kipper.

THE REVEREND SABINE BARING-GOULD

The Reverend Sabine Baring-Gould,
  Rector (sometime) at Lew,
Once at a Christmas party asked,
  'Whose pretty child are you?'

(The Rector's family was long,
  His memory was poor,
And as to who was who had grown
  Increasingly unsure.)

At this, the infant on the stair
  Most sorrowfully sighed.
'Whose pretty little girl am I?
  Why, *yours*, papa!' she cried.

The Reverend Sabine Baring-Gould (1834–1924) was Rector for 43 years at Lewtrenchard in Devon. He is the author of the hymn 'Onward, Christian soldiers'.

SEXTON, RING THE CURFEW

Sexton, ring the curfew,
Make the tower sway,
Tell all the children
To come from play.

Ring the bell, sexton,
That everyone may know
It's time for the children
To homeward go.

Here comes Betty,
Here comes May,
Here comes Hetty
Been missing all day.

Here comes Lily,
Here comes Lee,
Here comes Billy
With a cut on his knee.

Here comes Abel,
Here comes Hope,
Here comes Mabel
With a skipping rope.

Here comes Zacky,
Here comes Luke,
Here comes Jackie
With his nose in a book.

Here comes Polly,
Here comes Ruth,
Here comes Molly
With an aching tooth.

Here comes Evie,
Here comes Flo,
Here comes Stevie
With a twisted toe.

Here comes Theo,
Here comes Franz,
Here comes Leo
With a hole in his pants.

Here comes Zoë,
Here comes Jane,
And here's little Joey,
Last again.

When I was a child in my home-town of Launceston the curfew bell (a memory of Norman times) was still rung in the parish church tower for five minutes just after 8 p.m.

MRS BESSIE BUSYBODY

Mrs Bessie Busybody,
I declare,
Knows all the news
And some to spare.

From six in the morning
On the dot
Peers through the window
To see what's what.

Who's up early?
Who's up late?
Who wrote that
On the schoolyard gate?

Who's getting better?
Who's getting worse?
Who's had a visit
From the District Nurse?

Who turned the dustbins
Upside down?
Who had a call
From P.C. Brown?

Who wasn't home
Till twelve last night?
Who broke his nose
In a fisticuff fight?

Who cracked the glass
In the garden frame?
Who didn't answer
When the rent-man came?

Who climbed the wall
At Number Five,
Took all the honey
Out of the hive,

Then as cool
As cool could be
Stole every apple
From the orchard tree?

Who let the bulldog
Off his chain?
Who had a case
Of best champagne?

Who's gone missing,
And who is due
To have a little baby
In a month or two?

Winter, spring-time,
Summer-time, fall,
Mrs Bessie Busybody
Knows it all.

COLONEL FAZACKERLEY

Colonel Fazackerley Butterworth-Toast
Bought an old castle complete with a ghost,
But someone or other forgot to declare
To Colonel Fazack that the spectre was there.

On the very first evening, while waiting to dine,
The Colonel was taking a fine sherry wine,
When the ghost, with a furious flash and a flare,
Shot out of the chimney and shivered, 'Beware!'

Colonel Fazackerley put down his glass
And said, 'My dear fellow, that's really first class!
I just can't conceive how you do it at all.
I imagine you're going to a Fancy Dress Ball?'

At this, the dread ghost gave a withering cry.
Said the Colonel (his monocle firm in his eye),
'Now just how you do it I wish I could think.
Do sit down and tell me, and please have a drink.'

The ghost in his phosphorous cloak gave a roar
And floated about between ceiling and floor.
He walked through a wall and returned through a pane
And backed up the chimney and came down again.

Said the Colonel, 'With laughter I'm feeling quite weak!'
(As trickles of merriment ran down his cheek).
'My house-warming party I hope you won't spurn.
You *must* say you'll come and you'll give us a turn!'

Whereupon, the poor spectre – quite out of his wits –
Proceeded to shake himself almost to bits.
He rattled his chains and he clattered his bones
And he filled the whole castle with mumbles and moans.

But Colonel Fazackerley, just as before,
Was simply delighted and called out, 'Encore!'
At which the ghost vanished, his efforts in vain,
And never was seen at the castle again.

'Oh dear, what a pity!' said Colonel Fazack.
'I don't know his name, so I can't call him back.'
And then with a smile that was hard to define,
Colonel Fazackerley went in to dine.

ONE DAY AT A PERRANPORTH PET-SHOP

One day at a Perranporth pet-shop
  On a rather wild morning in June,
A lady from Par bought a budgerigar
  And she sang to a curious tune:
'Say that you love me, my sweetheart,
  My darling, my dovey, my pride,
My very own jewel, my dear one!'
  'Oh lumme,' the budgie replied.

'I'll feed you entirely on cream-cakes
  And doughnuts all smothered in jam,
And puddings and pies of incredible size,
  And peaches and melons and ham.
And you shall drink whiskies and sodas,
  For comfort your cage shall be famed.
You shall sleep in a bed lined with satin.'
  'Oh crikey!' the budgie exclaimed.

But the lady appeared not to hear him
  For she showed neither sorrow nor rage,
As with common-sense tardy and action foolhardy
  She opened the door of his cage.
'Come perch on my finger, my honey,
  To show you are mine, O my sweet!' –
Whereupon the poor fowl with a shriek and a howl
  Took off like a jet down the street.

And high he flew up above Cornwall
  To ensure his escape was no failure,
Then his speed he increased and he flew south and east
  To his ancestral home in Australia,
For although to the folk of that country
  The word 'budgerigar' means 'good food',
He said, 'I declare I'll feel much safer there
  Than in Bodmin or Bugle or Bude.'

ENVOI

And I'm sure with the budgie's conclusion
  You all will agree without fail:
Best eat frugal and free in a far-distant tree
  Than down all the wrong diet in jail.

LION

That's Saint Jerome, my master, over there
Writing a book in Latin. All of five
Years he's been at it. The two of us share
A lodging in this shabby desert cave.

Most folk find him a bit cantankerous.
Tongue like a knife. Gets in an awful tear
With scholars, pilgrims seeking his advice
And (worst of all) tourists who come to stare.

But here I must make one thing very plain:
This wise man has a heart as well as head.
Long years ago he eased a giant thorn
Out of my paw, while other people fled.

He watched, he tended me, quite unafraid,
Till once again I could both race and run,
And then it was a serious vow I made:
I would protect him till my life was done.

I've surely got my work cut out. But then,
I sleep with open eyes, as you will see
In paintings of us by quite famous men,
Although at first you may not notice me.

Sometimes he beats his breast with a flat stone.
Sometimes he gives a very little groan.
(I can't think why.) Well, be that as it may,
To all who call on him from near, from far:
Treat this great scholar with respect, I say.
            Grrrrrr!

Saint Jerome lived from about 342 to 420 AD. He translated most of the Bible
from its original languages into Latin.

In earlier times the lion was thought to sleep with its eyes open and so to be at
all times watchful and alert.

FRANCESCO DE LA VEGA

Francesco de la Vega
From the hours of childhood
Passed his days
In the salt of the ocean.

Only one word he spoke.
Lierjanes! – the name
Of the sea-village of his birth
In the Year of God 1657.

While other children
Helped in field or kitchen,
Wandered the mountain-slope,
He swam the wild bay.

While others were at church
He dived to where lobster and squid
Lodged in the sea's dark cellar.
He must suffer a salt death, said Father Ramiro.

His mother and father entreated him
To come to his own bed.
His brothers and sisters called him
Home from the yellow sand-bar.

Amazed, they watched him
Arrow the waves like a young dolphin.
Until they tired of waiting, he hid
Under the mountain of black water.

On a night mad with storm
The waves rose high as the church-tower
And beat the shore like a drum.
He did not return with the morning.

Foolish boy, now he is drowned, they said.
His family added their salt tears to the ocean
As they cast on flowers and prayers.
In my opinion, he asked for it, said Father Ramiro.

Years flowed by: ten, twenty.
The village of Lierjanes forgot him.
Then, miles off Cadiz, herring fishermen
Sighted, at dawning, a sea-creature.

Three days they pursued him
Through the autumn waters;
Trapped him at last in strong nets
And brought him to land.

They gazed at his silver body in wonder;
At his pale eyes, staring always ahead;
At his hair, tight, and as a red moss.
What seemed like bright scales adorned his spine.

Most marvellous of all, instead
Of nails upon his feet and hands
There grew strange shells
That glowed gently like jewels of the sea.

When they questioned him
All he would reply was, *Lierjanes!*
Wrapping him in a soft white sailcloth
They laid him on a bed of linen.

A monk of Cadiz heard their story.
It is Francesco de la Vega,
The fish-boy of Lierjanes, he declared.
I shall bring him to his home and family.

Ah, but how his parents, brothers, sisters
Wept with happiness and welcomed him
With loving kisses and embraces, as though
Like Lazarus he had risen, and from a sea-grave!

But the young man returned no sign
Of love or recognition.
He gazed at them as though sightless;
Was indifferent to their sighs, their fondlings.

Long years he dwelt among them,
Never speaking, eating little,
Shifting unhappily in the decent clothes
With which they arrayed him.

One morning, nine years on,
He vanished from the house and hearth-side;
Was seen no more in the village of Lierjanes.
Great was the sadness of those who loved him!

Months, years ahead, two fishermen
Hauling across the stubborn waters
Of the Bay of Asturias
Sighted a sudden sea-creature at play.

Swiftly, and with spear and net,
They followed, but he escaped them.
As he rushed through the waves they heard a cry.
Lierjanes! Lierjanes!

Nursery Rhyme of Innocence

and Experience

I had a silver penny
  And an apricot tree
And I said to the sailor
  On the white quay

'Sailor O sailor
  Will you bring me
If I give you my penny
  And my apricot tree

'A fez from Algeria
  An Arab drum to beat
A little gilt sword
  And a parakeet?'

And he smiled and he kissed me
  As strong as death
And I saw his red tongue
  And I felt his sweet breath

'You may keep your penny
And your apricot tree
And I'll bring your presents
Back from sea.'

O the ship dipped down
On the rim of the sky
And I waited while three
Long summers went by

Then one steel morning
On the white quay
I saw a grey ship
Come in from sea

Slowly she came
Across the bay
For her flashing rigging
Was shot away

All round her wake
The seabirds cried
And flew in and out
Of the hole in her side

Slowly she came
In the path of the sun
And I heard the sound
Of a distant gun

And a stranger came running
   Up to me
From the deck of the ship
   And he said, said he

'O are you the boy
   Who would wait on the quay
With the silver penny
   And the apricot tree?

'I've a plum-coloured fez
   And a drum for thee
And a sword and a parakeet
   From over the sea.'

'O where is the sailor
   With bold red hair?
And what is that volley
   On the bright air?

'O where are the other
   Girls and boys?
And why have you brought me
   Children's toys?'

FROST ON THE FLOWER

Frost on the flower,
Leaf and frond,
Snow on the field-path,
Ice on the pond.

Out of the east
A white wind comes.
Hail on the rooftop
Kettledrums.

Snow-fog wanders
Hollow and hill.
Along the valley
The stream is still.

Thunder and lightning.
Down slaps the rain.
No doubt about it.
Summer again.

HERE WE GO ROUND THE ROUND HOUSE

Here we go round the Round House
In the month of one,
Looking to the eastward
For the springing sun.
The sky is made of ashes,
The trees are made of bone,
And all the water in the well
Is stubborn as a stone.

Here we go round the Round House
In the month of two,
Waiting for the weather
To thaw my dancing shoe.
In St Thomas River
Hide the freckled trout,
But for dinner on Friday
I shall pull one out.

Here we go round the Round House
In the month of three,
Listening for the bumble
Of the humble-bee.
The light is growing longer,
The geese begin to lay,
The song-thrush in the churchyard
Charms the cold away.

Here we go round the Round House
In the month of four,
Watching a couple dressed in green
Dancing through the door.
One wears a wreath of myrtle,
Another, buds of thorn:
God grant that all men's children
Be as sweetly born.

Here we go round the Round House
In the month of five,
Waiting for the summer
To tell us we're alive.
All round the country
The warm seas flow,
The devil's on an ice-cap
Melting with the snow.

Here we go round the Round House
In the month of six;
High in the tower
The town clock ticks.
Hear the black quarter-jacks
Beat the noon bell;
They say the day is half away
And the year as well.

Here we go round the Round House
In the month of seven,
The river running thirsty
From Cornwall to Devon.
The sun is on the hedgerow,
The cattle in the stream,
And one will give us strawberries
And one will give us cream.

Here we go round the Round House
In the month of eight,
Hoping that for harvest
We shall never wait.
Slyly the sunshine
Butters up the bread
To bear us through the winter
When the light is dead.

Here we go round the Round House
In the month of nine,
Watching the orchard apple
Turning into wine.
The day after tomorrow
I'll take one from the tree
And pray the worm will do no harm
If it comes close to me.

Here we go round the Round House
In the month of ten,
While the cattle winter
In the farmer's pen.
Thick the leaves are lying
On the coppice floor;
Such a coat against the cold
Never a body wore.

Here we go round the Round House
In the month of eleven,
The sea-birds swiftly flying
To the coast of heaven.
The plough is in the furrow,
The boat is on the strand;
May I be fed on fish and bread
While water lies on land.

Here we go round the Round House
In the month of twelve,
The hedgers break the brier
And the ditchers delve.
As we go round the Round House
May the moon and sun
Guide us to tomorrow
And the month of one:
And life be never done.

The Round House, c.1830, is built over a broken market cross at Launceston, in Cornwall.

FIGGIE HOBBIN

Nightingales' tongues, your majesty?
  Quails in aspic, cost a purse of money?
Oysters from the deep, raving sea?
  Grapes and Greek honey?
Beads of black caviare from the Caspian?
  Rock melon with corn on the cob in?
Take it all away! grumbled the old King of Cornwall.
  Bring me some figgie hobbin![1]

Devilled lobster, your majesty?
  Scots kail brose or broth?
Grilled mackerel with gooseberry sauce?
  Cider ice that melts in your mouth?
Pears filled with nut and date salad?
  Christmas pudding with a tanner or a bob in?[2]
Take it all away! groused the old King of Cornwall.
  Bring me some figgie hobbin!

Amber jelly, your majesty?
  Passion fruit flummery?
Pineapple sherbet, milk punch or Pavlova cake,
  Sugary, summery?
Carpet-bag steak, blueberry grunt, cinnamon
    crescents?
  Spaghetti as fine as the thread on a bobbin?
Take it all away! grizzled the old King of Cornwall.
  Bring me some figgie hobbin!

So in from the kitchen came figgie hobbin,
    Shining and speckled with raisins sweet,
And though on the King of Cornwall's land
    The rain it fell and the wind it beat,
As soon as a forkful of figgie hobbin
    Up to his lips he drew,
Over the palace a pure sun shone
    And the sky was blue.
THAT'S *what I wanted*! he smiled, his face
    Now as bright as the breast of the robin.
To cure the sickness of the heart, ah –
    Bring me some figgie hobbin!

¹ Figgie hobbin is a Cornish pudding sweetened with raisins, which are known as 'figs' in Cornwall. It may be eaten either with meat, or (with the addition of more raisins) as a sweet.   ² A tanner and a bob were slang for sixpence (2½p) and a shilling (5p) in 'old' money.

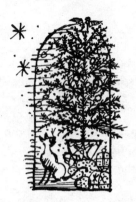

THEY'RE FETCHING IN IVY AND HOLLY

'They're fetching in ivy and holly
And putting it this way and that.
I simply can't think of the reason,'
Said Si-Si the Siamese cat.

'They're pinning up lanterns and streamers.
There's mistletoe over the door.
They've brought in a tree from the garden.
I do wish I knew what it's for.

'It's covered with little glass candles
That go on and off without stop.
They've put it to stand in a corner
And tied up a fairy on top.

'They're stringing bright cards by the dozen
And letting them hang in a row.
Some people outside in the roadway
Are singing a song in the snow.

'I saw all the children write letters
And – I'm not at all sure this was wise –
They posted each one *up the chimney*.
I couldn't believe my own eyes.

'What on earth, in the middle of winter,
Does the family think it is at?
Won't somebody please come and tell me?'
Said Si-Si the Siamese cat.

EARLY IN THE MORNING

Early in the morning
The water hits the rocks,
The birds are making noises
Like old alarum clocks,
The soldier on the skyline
Fires a golden gun
And over the back of the chimney-stack
Explodes the silent sun.

THE OWL LOOKED OUT OF THE IVY BUSH

The owl looked out of the ivy bush
And he solemnly said, said he,
'If you want to live an owlish life
Be sure you are not like me.

'When the sun goes down and the moon comes up
And the sky turns navy blue,
I'm certain to go tu-whoo tu-whit
Instead of tu-whit tu-whoo.

'And even then nine times out of ten
(And it's absolutely true)
I somehow go out of my owlish mind
With a whit-tu whoo-tu too.'

'There's nothing in water,' said the owl,
'In air or on the ground
With a kindly word for the sort of bird
That sings the wrong way round.'

'I might,' wept the owl in the ivy bush,
'Be just as well buried and dead.
You can bet your boots no one gives two hoots!'
'Do I, friend my,' I said.

OLD MRS THING-UM-E-BOB

Old Mrs Thing-um-e-bob,
  Lives at you-know-where,
Dropped her what-you-may-call-it down
  The well of the kitchen stair.

'Gracious me!' said Thing-um-e-bob,
  'This don't look too bright.
I'll ask old Mr What's-his-name
  To try and put it right.'

Along came Mr What's-his-name,
  He said, 'You've broke the lot!
I'll have to see what I can do
  With some of the you-know-what.'

So he gave the what-you-may-call-it a pit
  And he gave it a bit of a pat,
And he put it all together again
  With a little of this and that.

And he gave the what-you-may-call-it a dib
  And he gave it a dab as well
When all of a sudden he heard a note
  As clear as any bell.

'It's as good as new!' cried What's-his-name.
  'But please remember, now,
In future Mrs Thing-um-e-bob
  You'll have to go you-know-how.'

ANNABEL-EMILY

Annabel-Emily Huntington-Horne
Who lives at Threepenny Cam
From the very first moment that she was born
Would eat nothing whatever but jam.

They offered her milk, they offered her bread,
They offered her biscuits and beans
But Annabel-Emily shook her head
And made the most horrible scenes.

They offered her chicken, and also a choice
Of sausage or cheese or Spam[1]
But Annabel screamed at the top of her voice,
'Can't you see what I'm wanting is JAM?'

Her parents they wept like the watery bay
And they uttered and spluttered such cries
As, 'She's perfectly certain to waste away
In front of our very own eyes!'

But Annabel-Emily Huntington-Horne,
Her hair the colour of snow,
Still lives in the cottage where she was born
A hundred years ago.

Her tooth is as sugary sweet today
As ever it was before
And as for her hundred years, they say
She's good for a hundred more.

She's pots of apricot, strawberry, peach
In twos and threes and fours
On yards and yards of shelves that reach
From the ceilings to the floors.

She's jars of currants red and black
On every chest and chair
And plum and gooseberry in a stack
On every step of the stair.

Raspberry, cranberry, blackberry, or
Apple, damson, quince –
There never was better jam before
Nor will ever be better since.

For Annabel of Threepenny Cam,
Whose ways are quite well known,
Has never been one for boughten[2] jam
And always makes her own.

But if, when you are passing by,
She invites you for tea and a treat
Be careful just how you reply
If your taste and tooth aren't sweet:

Or it's certain (all the neighbours warn)
You'll be in a terrible jam
With Annabel-Emily Huntington-Horne
Who lives at Threepenny Cam.

[1] 'Spam' is the proprietary name for a particular brand of tinned, spiced ham loaf which first became well known in Britain during the Second World War.

[2] 'Boughten' is a dialect word meaning something bought in a shop as opposed to being home-made.

TAVISTOCK GOOSE FAIR

The day my father took me to the Fair
Was just before he died of the First War.
We walked the damp, dry-leaved October air.
My father was twenty-seven and I was four.

The train was whistles and smoke and dirty steam.
I won myself a smudge of soot in the eye.
He tricked it out as we sat by a windy stream.
Farmers and gypsies were drunken-dancing by.

My dad wore his Irish cap, his riding-coat.
His boots and leggings shone as bright as a star.
He carried an ashling stick, stood soldier-straight.
The touch of his hand was strong as an iron bar.

The roundabout played 'Valencia' on the Square.
I heard the frightened geese in a wicker pen.
Out of his mouth an Indian man blew fire.
There was a smell of beer; cold taste of rain.

The cheapjacks bawled best crockery made of bone,
Solid silver spoons and cures for a cold.
My father bought a guinea for half-a-crown.
The guinea was a farthing painted gold.

Everyone else was tall. The sky went black.
My father stood me high on a drinking-trough.
I saw a man in chains escape from a sack.
I bothered in case a gypsy carried me off.

Today, I hardly remember my father's face;
Only the shine of his boot-and-legging leather
The day we walked the yellow October weather;
Only the way he strode at a soldier's pace,
The way he stood like a soldier of the line;
Only the feel of his iron hand on mine.

The Fair is still held every year at this Devonshire town on the second Wednesday
in October.

By St Thomas Water

By St Thomas Water
Where the river is thin
We looked for a jam-jar
To catch the quick fish in.
Through St Thomas Churchyard
Jessie and I ran
The day we took the jam-pot
Off the dead man.

On the scuffed tombstone
The grey flowers fell,
Cracked was the water,
Silent the shell.
The snake for an emblem
Swirled on the slab,
Across the beach of sky the sun
Crawled like a crab.

'If we walk,' said Jessie,
'Seven times round,
We shall hear a dead man
Speaking underground.'
Round the stone we danced, we sang,
Watched the sun drop,
Laid our heads and listened
At the tomb-top.

Soft as the thunder
At the storm's start
I heard a voice as clear as blood,
Strong as the heart.
But what words were spoken
I can never say,
I shut my fingers round my head,
Drove them away.

'What are those letters, Jessie,
Cut so sharp and trim
All round this holy stone
With earth up to the brim?'
Jessie traced the letters
Black as coffin-lead.
'He is not dead but sleeping,'
Slowly she said.

I looked at Jessie,
Jessie looked at me,
And our eyes in wonder
Grew wide as the sea.
Past the green and bending stones
We fled hand in hand,
Silent through the tongues of grass
To the river strand.

By the creaking cypress
We moved as soft as smoke
For fear all the people
Underneath awoke.
Over all the sleepers
We darted light as snow
In case they opened up their eyes,
Called us from below.

Many a day has faltered
Into many a year
Since the dead awoke and spoke
And we would not hear.
Waiting in the cold grass
Under a crinkled bough,
Quiet stone, cautious stone,
What do you tell me now?

TAM SNOW

(to Kaye Webb)

Who in the white wood
Barefoot, ice-fingered,
Runs to and fro?
    Tam Snow.

Who, soft as a ghost,
Falls on our house to strike
Blow after blow?
    Tam Snow.

Who with a touch of the hand
Stills the world's sound
In its flow?
    Tam Snow.

Who holds to our side,
Though as friend or as foe
We never may know?
    Tam Snow.

Who hides in the hedge
After thaw, waits for more
Of his kind to show?
    Tam Snow.

Who is the guest
First we welcome, then
Long to see go?
    Tam Snow.

I HAD A LITTLE CAT

I had a little cat called Tim Tom Tay,
I took him to town on market day,
I combed his whiskers, I brushed his tail,
I wrote on a label, 'Cat for Sale.
Knows how to deal with rats and mice.
Two pounds fifty. Bargain price.'

But when the people came to buy
I saw such a look in Tim Tom's eye
That it was clear as clear could be
I couldn't sell Tim for a fortune's fee.
I was shamed and sorry, I'll tell you plain,
And I took home Tim Tom Tay again.

Let Us Walk to the Williwaw Islands

'Let us walk to the Williwaw Islands,'
Said the porcupine-pig to the snoar.
'If we turn to the right by the Isle of Wight
We'll be there by a quarter to four.'

'Never once have I gazed on the ocean,'
Said the snoar to the porcupine-pig.
'How I wish I could stray through its waters one day!
But isn't it awfully *big*?

'And I've heard that the waves of the briny
Are inclined to be salty and steep
Should one venture out more than ten yards from the
        shore –
And isn't it frightfully deep?'

'I can't think,' then replied his companion,
'Where you get such ideas, and that's flat.
A very old spoof who once sat on the roof
Told me something quite different from that.

'He remarked that the bright-bluey water
Stood quite still in the stiffest of breeze,
And the sea-salty waste had a sugary taste
And barely came up to one's knees.

'And he said that the Williwaw Islands
Are constructed of coconut cream
And Belgian chocs and peppermint rocks
And orange-and-lemonade streams.'

'I foresee both our lives very shortly
Becoming a terrible bore.
Time to get off the shelf! Find things out for oneself!'
Said the porcupine-pig to the snoar.

'On reflection, my dearest old crony,
I can do nothing more than agree.
Let us hurry away without further delay,'
Said the snoar to the porcupine-p.

So they packed up their goods and their chattels
(Whatever a chattel may be),
Some biscuits and bread and a buttery spread
And they hurried away to the sea.

But when, at the edge of the ocean,
They gazed at its foam and its fret,
Said the snoar, 'Gracious me, my friend porcupine-p.,
It's the frightfullest thing I've seen yet!'

For the water it tumbled and twisted
And jumped up right out of the bay,
And it just wasn't true that its colour was blue
But a horrible sort of a grey.

It wouldn't stand still for a moment.
It did nothing but surge and then swell.
It held a big ship in its watery grip
And it broke pieces off it as well.

Said the porcupine-pig, 'I've a feeling
As I gaze at the sea and the skies
That to walk all those miles to the Williwaw Isles
Might turn out to be rather unwise.'

And the snoar, who was sensibly smiling,
He lifted a sensible thumb,
And they turned in their track and they made their way
     back
The very same way they had come.

'We don't care for candy,' they chanted.
'Nor for sweets nor for treats large or small,
But if there's a spoof resting up on your roof
We'd be glad if you gave us a call, that's all.
We'd be glad if you gave us a call.'

FAMILY ALBUM

I wish I liked Aunt Leonora
When she draws in her breath with a hiss
And with fingers of ice and a grip like a vice
She gives me a walloping kiss.

I wish I loved Uncle Nathaniel
(The one with the teeth and the snore).
He's really a pain when he tells me *again*
About what he did in the War.

I really don't care for Aunt Millie,
Her bangles and brooches and beads,
Or the gun that she shoots or those ex-army boots
Or the terrible dogs that she breeds.

I simply can't stand Uncle Albert.
Quite frankly, he fills me with dread
When he gives us a tune with a knife, fork and
    spoon.
(I don't think he's right in the head.)

I wish I loved Hetty and Harry
(Aunt Hilary's horrible twins)
As they lie in their cots giving off lots and lots
Of gurgles and gargles and grins.

As for nieces or nephews or cousins
There seems nothing else one can do
Except sit in a chair and exchange a cold stare
As if we came out of a zoo.

Though they say blood is thicker than water,
I'm not at all certain it's so.
If you think it's the case, kindly write to this space.
It's something I'm anxious to know.

If we only could choose our relations
How happy, I'm certain, we'd be!
And just one thing more: I am perfectly sure
Mine all feel the same about me.

LEONARDO

Leonardo, painter, taking
  Morning air
    On Market Street
Saw the wild birds in their cages
  Silent in
    The dust, the heat.

Took his purse from out his pocket
  Never questioning
    The fee,
Bore the cages to the green shade
  Of a hill-top
    Cypress tree.

'What you lost,' said Leonardo,
  'I now give to you
    Again,
Free as noon and night and morning,
  As the sunshine,
    As the rain.'

And he took them from their prisons,
  Held them to
    The air, the sky;
Pointed them to the bright heaven.
  'Fly!' said Leonardo.
    'Fly!'

The story is told of the Italian painter Leonardo da Vinci (1452–1519).

MY NAME IS LITTLE MOSIE

My name is Little Mosie,
I lie among the bushes,
My cradle is a sailing-boat
Of yellow reeds and rushes.

It was my sister brought me
Beside the swimming water.
One morning very early came
The King of Egypt's daughter.

She took me to her palace,
She laid me in her bed,
She dressed me in the finest shirt
Of gold and silver thread.

She put a circlet on my brow,
A ring upon my hand,
'And you shall be,' she said to me,
'A Prince of Egypt land.'

But now, in a far country,
I tend my field-flock well
And none there is to listen
To the mystery I tell:

When I was Little Mosie
I lay among the bushes
Cradled in a sailing-boat
Of yellow reeds and rushes.

What Has Happened to Lulu?

What has happened to Lulu, mother?
    What has happened to Lu?
There's nothing in her bed but an old rag-doll
    And by its side a shoe.

Why is her window wide, mother,
    The curtain flapping free,
And only a circle on the dusty shelf
    Where her money-box used to be?

Why do you turn your head, mother,
    And why do the tear-drops fall?
And why do you crumple that note on the fire
    And say it is nothing at all?

I woke to voices late last night,
    I heard an engine roar.
Why do you tell me the things I heard
    Were a dream and nothing more?

I heard somebody cry, mother,
    In anger or in pain,
But now I ask you why, mother,
    You say it was a gust of rain.

Why do you wander about as though
    You don't know what to do?
What has happened to Lulu, mother?
    What has happened to Lu?

ZOW-BUG

Zow-bug, zow-bug
Under the stone,
One of a hundred
Or one on your own,
Hurrying, flurrying
To and fro,
Fourteen legs
On the go, go, go,
Why are you hiding
Out of the light?
Waiting for day
To turn to night.

Zow-bug, zow-bug
Scurrying through
A world of dusk
And a world of dew,
Now that you've left
Your house of wood
Is it bad you are up to
Or is it good
Down in the garden
Dark and deep?
Taking a turn
Round the compost heap.

Zow-bug, zow-bug
By the long shore
Tell me who
You are waiting for:
Is it King Neptune,
A sole or a dab,
A Cornish pilchard
Or an ocean crab?
Who will you meet
On Newlyn Quay?
             My great-great-grandaddy
             Lives in the sea.

CHARITY CHADDER

Charity Chadder
Borrowed a ladder,
Leaned it against the moon,
Climbed to the top
Without a stop
On the 31st of June,
Brought down every single star,
Kept them all in a pickle jar.

Zow-bug (sow-bug) is the country name for the woodlouse, a land-living
crustacean distantly related to the crab.

MAGGIE DOOLEY

Old Maggie Dooley
Twice a day
Comes to the Park
To search for the stray,
Milk in a bowl,
Scraps on a tray,
'Breakfast time!' 'Supper time!'
Hear her say.

Alone on a bench
She'll sit and wait
Till out of the bushes
They hesitate:
Tommy No-Tail
And Sammy No-Fur,
Half-Eye Sally
And Emmy No-Purr.

She sits by the children's
Roundabout
And takes a sip
From a bottle of stout.
She smiles a smile
And nods her head
Until her little
Family's fed.

Whatever the weather,
Shine or rain,
She comes at eight
And eight again.
'It's a Saint you are,'
To Maggie I said,
But she smiled a smile
And shook her head.

'Tom and Sammy,
Sally and Em,
They need me
And I need them.
I need them
And they need me.
That's all there is,'
She said, said she.

JACK THE TREACLE EATER

Here comes Jack the Treacle Eater,
Never swifter, never sweeter,
With a peck of messages,
Some long, some shorter,
From my Lord and Master's quarter
(Built like a minaret)
Somewhere in Somerset.
> *Jack, how do you make such speed*
> *From banks of Tone to banks of Tweed*
> *And all the way back?*
> 'I train on treacle,' says Jack.

Here's one for Sam Snoddy
(Cantankerous old body).
'Will you come for Christmas dinner
With Missus and Squire?'
'Not on your life,' says Sam.
'Rather eat bread and jam
By my own fire.'
> *Jack, how do you trot so spry*
> *The long road to Rye*
> *Bearing that heavy pack?*
> 'I train on treacle,' says Jack.

The original Jack lived in Somerset and was a famous runner who took messages
to and from London for the Messiter family of Barwick Park, near Yeovil. He
is said to have trained on treacle, and is commemorated there by one of four
follies (useless but usually delightful and expensive buildings put up for fun)
built by George Messiter in the early nineteenth century. On top of Jack's Folly

Here's one for Sally Bent
Lives in a gypsy tent
Down at Land's End.
'Will you sing at my daughter's bridal?'
'No,' says Sally. 'I'm too idle.
Besides, I've not much choice
Since up to Bodmin I lost my voice.'

> *Jack, how do you travel so light*
> *From morning star through half the*
> *night*
> *With never a snack?*
> 'I train on treacle,' says Jack.

Here's one for Trooper Slaughter,
Retired, of Petherwin Water.
'Dear Tom, will you come
And we'll talk of our days with the drum,
Bugle, fife and the cannon's thunder.'
'Too late,' says Tom, 'old chum.
I'm already six feet under.'

> *Jack, how do you care for your wife*
> *If you run all the days of your life?*
> *Is it something the rest of us lack?*
> 'I train on treacle,' says Jack.

is a figure of Hermes (representing Jack), the Greek messenger and herald of the gods. At midnight, Jack is said to climb down from his Folly and go to the lake by the great house in order to quench his tremendous thirst caused by eating so much treacle.

MRS MALARKEY

Mrs Malarkey
(Miss Rooke, that was)
Climbed to the top of a tree
And while she was there
The birds of the air
Kept her company.

Her friends and her family
Fretted and fumed
And did nothing but scold and sneer
But Mrs Malarkey
She smiled and said,
'I'm perfectly happy up here.

'In this beautiful nest
Of sticks and straw
I'm warmer by far than you,
And there's neither rent
Nor rates to pay
And a quite indescribable view.

'A shield from the snow
And the sun and rain
Are the leaves that grow me round.
I feel safer by far
On this green, green spar
Than ever I did on the ground.'

Mrs Malarkey
She covered herself
With feathers of purple and blue.
She flapped a wing
And began to sing
And she whistled and warbled too.

And the birds of the air
Brought seed and grain
And acorns and berries sweet,
And (I must confirm)
The occasional worm
As an extra special treat.

'Mrs Malarkey!
Come you down!'
The people all cried on the street.
But, *Chirrupy, chirrup*
She softly sang,
And, *Tweet, tweet,*
Tweet, tweet, tweet.
Chirrupy, chirrup
(As smooth as syrup)
And, *Tweet, tweet,*
Tweet, tweet, tweet.

LUCY LOVE'S SONG

I love a boy in Boulder,
I love a boy in Kew,
I love a boy in Bangalore
And one in Timbuktu.

I love a boy in Bari,
I love a boy in Rhyll,
I love a boy in Medicine Hat
And also in Seville.

I love a boy in Brooklyn,
I love a boy in Lille,
I love a boy in Alice Springs,
I love a boy in Kiel.

I love a boy in Ballarat,
I love a boy in Hayle,
I love a boy in Yellowknife,
I love a boy in Yale.

I love a boy in Buda,
I love a boy in Pest,
I love a boy in Trincomalee,
I love a boy in Brest.

I love a boy in Brisbane,
I love a boy in Ayr,
I love a boy in Aldershot,
I love a boy in Clare.

I love a boy in Augusta
In the State of Maine,
But the boy I love the best of all
Lives just along the lane.

WILLOUGHBY

Willoughby Whitebody-Barrington-Trew
Could never decide what the weather would do.
Out of his window he'd gaze by the hour
To see if it might be a shine or a shower.
He'd open the closet that's under the stair
And he'd hem and he'd haw as to what he should
    wear,
And often as not (and I'm stating a fact)
By the time he set off it was time to come back.

He'd wait by the hat-stand inside the front door
And ask himself hundreds of questions, or more.
'Will it snow? Will it blow? Will it rain? Will it hail?
Will these summery breezes turn into a gale?
Is the temperature likely to rise or to fall?
Do you think that we're in for a bit of a squall?
Although the sun's shining,' he'd say with a groan,
'It'll come down in buckets before I get home.'

'Shall I get me a waterproof? Put on a coat?
An ulster that buttons right up to my throat?
A bowler? A beret? A felt or a straw?
The finest glengarry that ever you saw?
Am I needing a panama hat or a cane?
A carriage-umbrella to keep off the rain?
Is it Wellington weather or sandal or shoe?
I'm ashamed to confess that I haven't a clue.
There's no doubt about it,' said Willoughby White,
'Whatever I do I just can't get it right –
And if folk say I'm crazy I don't care a jot,
So I might as well go out dressed up in the lot.'

And every item in closet and hall
He took until nothing was left there at all.
'You may sneer,' declared Willoughby, 'or you may
    scoff,
But if it's too hot you can take something off.'
And he'd say to himself till his breath was all gone,
'If you haven't it with you, you can't put it on.'
Said Willoughby Whitebody-Barrington who
Could never decide what the weather would do.

GOOD MORNING, MR CROCO-DOCO-DILE

Good morning, Mr Croco-doco-dile,
And how are you today?
I like to see you croco-smoco-smile
In your croco-woco-way.

From the tip of your beautiful croco-toco-tail
To your croco-hoco-head
You seem to me so croco-stoco-still
As if you're croco-doco-dead.

Perhaps if I touch your croco-cloco-claw
Or your croco-snoco-snout,
Or get up close to your croco-joco-jaw
I shall very soon find out.

But suddenly I croco-soco-see
In your croco-oco-eye
A curious kind of croco-gloco-gleam,
So I just don't think I'll try.

Forgive me, Mr Croco-doco-dile
But it's time I was away.
Let's talk a little croco-woco-while
Another croco-doco-day.

I Saw a Jolly Hunter

I saw a jolly hunter
  With a jolly gun
Walking in the country
  In the jolly sun.

In the jolly meadow
  Sat a jolly hare.
Saw the jolly hunter.
  Took jolly care.

Hunter jolly eager –
  Sight of jolly prey.
Forgot gun pointing
  Wrong jolly way.

Jolly hunter jolly head
  Over heels gone.
Jolly old safety-catch
  Not jolly on.

Bang went the jolly gun.
  Hunter jolly dead.
Jolly hare got clean away.
  Jolly good, I said.

THERE ONCE WAS A MAN

There once was a man
Called Knocketty Ned
Who wore his cat
On top of his head.
Upstairs, downstairs,
The whole world knew
Wherever he went
The cat went too.

He wore it at work,
He wore it at play,
He wore it to town
On market-day,
And for fear it should rain
Or the snowflakes fly
He carried a brolly
To keep it dry.

He never did fret
Nor fume because
He always knew
Just where it was.
'And when,' said Ned,
'In my bed I lie
There's no better nightcap
Money can buy.'

'There's no better bonnet
To be found,'
Said Knocketty Ned,
'The world around.
And furthermore
Was there ever a hat
As scared a mouse
Or scared a rat?'

Did ever you hear
Of a tale like that
As Knocketty Ned's
And the tale of his cat?

MR ZUKOVSKY

When Mr Augustus Zukovsky
First met his intended-to-be
His friends they all moaned and they grizzled and
      groaned,
'You just *can't* think of marrying she!
Why, she's clumsy, they say, as a camel
(If camels *are* clumsy, that is).
The mere thought of it, Mr Zukovsky,
Is fetching us all in a fizz!

'It looks as if what she is wearing
Was fired at her out of a gun,
And the state of her hair is her mother's despair
And like rays sticking out of the sun.
While as for you, Mr Zukovsky,
You're always so sober and neat,
And it's very well known how you brush and you comb
Before you set off down the street.

'She's a voice like the Seven Stones Lighthouse
When it's speaking of fogs or of gales,
And if she should whisper a secret
You can hear it from Windsor to Wales.
She's no ear whatever for music
And she can't tell a sharp from a flat.
When they're playing the National Anthem
She doesn't know what they are at.

'The money it slides through her fingers,
She can't sew, she can't clean, she can't cook,
And she spends half the day (so the neighbours all say)

With her nose in a *poetry* book.'
But to Mr Augustus Zukovsky
Such words were a slander and shame,
And he walked up the aisle with a beautiful smile
And he married his love just the same.

Now Mr and Mrs Zukovsky
For twenty-five years have been wed,
And there isn't a happier couple
In the whole of the kingdom, it's said.
They've a dog and two cats and five children,
A budgie, a buck and a doe,
And you won't find a jollier family
Though you search the world high and then low.

And as for those friends and companions
Who prophesied nothing but woe,
They all of them cry (without winking an eye),
'But we always *said* it would be so,
They're so awf'ly well suited, you know!
Yes, we always said it would be so,
We ALWAYS said it would be so, and so,
We *always* said it would be so.'

LORD LOVELACE

Lord Lovelace rode home from the wars,
His wounds were black as ice,
While overhead the winter sun
Hung out its pale device.

The lance was tattered in his hand,
Sundered his axe and blade,
And in a bloody coat of war
Lord Lovelace was arrayed.

And he was sick and he was sore
But never sad was he,
And whistled bright as any bird
Upon an April tree.

'Soon, soon,' he cried, 'at Lovelace Hall
Fair Ellen I shall greet,
And she with loving heart and hand
Will make my sharp wounds sweet.

'And Young Jehan the serving-man
Will bring the wine and bread,
And with a yellow link will light
Us to the bridal bed.'

But when he got to Lovelace Hall
Burned were both wall and stack,
And in the stinking moat the tower
Had tumbled on its back.

And none welcomed Lord Lovelace home
Within the castle shell,
And ravaged was the land about
That Lord Lovelace knew well.

Long in his stirrups Lovelace stood
Before his broken door,
And slowly rode he down the hill
Back to the bitter war.

Nor mercy showed he from that day,
Nor tear fell from his eye,
And rich and poor both fearful were
When Black Lovelace rode by.

This tale is true that now I tell
To woman and to man,
As Fair Ellen is my wife's name
And mine is Young Jehan.

TABITHA TUPPER

Tabitha Tupper
Had frogs for supper,
Joshua Jones had snails.
Fidelity Flutter
Had seaweed butter
(I think it comes from Wales).

Jeremy Croop
Had sting-nettle soup
Flavoured with gingerbread.
Dorothy Dart
Had fungus tart
With a kind of chocolate spread.

Timothy Lamb
Had jellyfish jam
Spread with Devonshire cream.
Christopher Hawke
Had bubble-and-squawk
(He said it tasted a dream).

Nathan Newell
Had winter gruel
That's made from curry and cheese.
William Wade
Had marmalade
Sprinkled with prunes and peas.

But sad to tell
They felt far from well
When they went up to bed,
And 'Why it's so
We just don't know!'
Their parents sighed and said,

While Tabitha Tupper
And all the others
Scarcely closed an eye,
And felt ever-so-slightly
Better-go-lightly,
And simply couldn't say why.

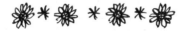

DANDELION

Dandelion,
Yellow crown,
Now your petals
All are gone,
Speak to me
The time of day
As I blow
Your seeds away.

If at one breath
They are flown
I need never
Hurry home,
But if any
Seeds remain
I must to
My home again.

Dandelion,
Yellow head,
Tell me when
I shall be wed.
Country clock
Without a chime
When shall be
My wedding time?

Dandelion,
Tell me fair
How many children
I shall bear,
Or tell me true
As moon or sun
If there shall be
Never a one.

Dandelion,
Flowering clear
Through the seasons
Of the year
Teach me simple,
Teach me slow
All these things
That I must know.

UNDER THE HAWTHORN

Under the hawthorn
The white witch dwells
Who held in her noddle
A hundred spells,
But now she is old
As night and day,
Her memory gone
Quite far away
And try as she might
A spell to find
She can't call a single
One to mind.

She beats with her palm
The crown of her head,
She mumbles, she grumbles
From breakfast to bed,
She snaps her fingers,
She cracks her thumbs,
She whistles and whimpers,
She haws and hums,
But never a spell
Can she sing or say
Though you wait for a year,
A month and a day.

Her five wits once
Were winter-bright
As she moved on her mopstick
Through the night
In her cloak of stars,
Her pointed hat,
And safe on her shoulder
Zal the cat,
But now she sits
As cold as a stone
Her flying days
All dead and done.

Her spells that were white
As the birch-tree wood
Are vanished away
And gone for good,
And still she scrapes
Her poor old brain
But there's none will tell her
It's all in vain
As she sits under
A failing sun.

Never a body.
Never a one.

A white witch was thought to practise only 'white' or beneficial magic.

How to Protect Baby from a Witch

Bring a bap
Of salted bread
To the pillow
At his head.
Hang a wreath
Of garlic strong
By the cradle
He lies on.
(Twelve flowers
On each stem
For Christ's good men
Of Bethlehem.)
Dress the baby's
Rocking-bed
With the rowan
Green and red.
(Wicked witch
Was never seen
By the rowan's
Red and green.)
Bring the crystal
Water in,
Let the holy
Words begin,
And the priest
Or parson now
Write a cross
Upon his brow.

STONE IN THE WATER

Stone in the water,
Stone on the sand,
Whom shall I marry
When I get to land?

Will he be handsome
Or will he be plain,
Strong as the sun
Or rich as the rain?

Will he be dark
Or will he be fair,
And what will be the colour
That shines in his hair?

Will he come late
Or will he come soon,
At morning or midnight
Or afternoon?

What will he say
Or what will he sing,
And will he be holding
A plain gold ring?

Stone in the water
Still and small,
Tell me if he comes,
Or comes not at all.

Newlyn Buildings

When we lived in Newlyn Buildings
Half a hundred years ago
Scents and sounds from every quarter
(Sometimes fast and sometimes slow)
Floated through the bricks and mortar.
Though who had the top apartment
No-one ever seemed to know.

On our left, the Widow Whiting
By a curtain fresh as snow
Sat with cotton and with needle
Working at a little treadle
Hard as ever she could go.
Though who had the top apartment
No-one ever seemed to know.

To our right was Catgut Johnson
With a fiddle and a bow,
Sometimes wrong and sometimes right time,
Morning, noon and often night-time
Playing to his tame white crow.
Though who had the top apartment
No-one ever seemed to know.

Underneath lived Annie Fluther,
Family washing all a-blow,
Image of the perfect mother,
Children neat from head to toe
(Six of one and six the other).
Though who had the top apartment
No-one ever seemed to know.

But I heard, in Newlyn Buildings,
Times and seasons long ago,
Overhead each day from dawning,
Through the night from dark to morning,
Footsteps pacing to and fro,
Footsteps old and footsteps new,
To and fro and fro and to.
Though who had the top apartment
No-one ever seemed to know.

My Mother Saw a Dancing Bear

My mother saw a dancing bear
By the schoolyard, a day in June.
The keeper stood with chain and bar
And whistle-pipe, and played a tune.

And bruin lifted up its head
And lifted up its dusty feet,
And all the children laughed to see
It caper in the summer heat.

They watched as for the Queen it died.
They watched it march. They watched it halt.
They heard the keeper as he cried,
'Now, roly-poly!' 'Somersault!'

And then, my mother said, there came
The keeper with a begging-cup,
The bear with burning coat of fur,
Shaming the laughter to a stop.

They paid a penny for the dance,
But what they saw was not the show;
Only, in bruin's aching eyes,
Far-distant forests, and the snow.

Green Man, Blue Man

As I was walking through Guildhall Square
I smiled to see a green man there,
But when I saw him coming near
My heart was filled with nameless fear.

As I was walking through Madford Lane
A blue man stood there in the rain.
I asked him in by my front-door,
For I'd seen a blue man before.

As I was walking through Landlake Wood
A grey man in the forest stood,
But when he turned and said, 'Good day'
I shook my head and ran away.

As I was walking by Church Stile
A purple man spoke there a while.
I spoke to him because, you see,
A purple man once lived by me.

But when the night falls dark and fell
How, O how, am I to tell,
Grey man, green man, purple, blue,
Which is which is which of you?

MY YOUNG MAN'S A CORNISHMAN

My young man's a Cornishman
He lives in Camborne town,
I met him going up the hill
As I was coming down.

His eye is bright as Dolcoath tin,
His body as china clay,
His hair is dark as Werrington Wood
Upon St Thomas's Day.

He plays the rugby football game
On Saturday afternoon,
And we shall walk on Wilsey Down
Under the bouncing moon.

My young man's a Cornishman,
Won't leave me in the lurch,
And one day we shall married be
Up to Trura church.[1]

He's bought me a ring of Cornish gold,
A belt of copper made,
At Bodmin Fair for my wedding-dress
A purse of silver paid.

And I shall give him scalded cream
And starry-gazy pie,[2]
And make him a saffron cake for tea
And a pasty for by and by.

My young man's a Cornishman,
A proper young man is he,
And a Cornish man with a Cornish maid
Is how it belongs to be.

[1] Truro Cathedral   [2] A starry-gazy pie is a fish pie, made of pilchards. The fish are cooked whole, with the heads piercing the crust as though gazing up to the heavens.

I WON'T GO HOME

I won't go home by the churchyard.
I know I'm sure to see
Wicked Willy Waters
Waiting there for me.

When there's never a light up in the sky
And the dark spreads like the sea
And the tawny owl goes *wick-e-wick*
In the dusky conker tree,

I know that Willy Waters,
Wrapped up in a big white sheet,
Is lying in wait by the churchyard gate
At the end of St Thomas Street.

He's fixed his face with whitewash,
His thumbs and fingers too,
And he'll shriek and he'll squall and he'll jump the wall
And cry out, 'Whoo-hoo-hoo!'

I won't mind ghosts or goblins
Or demons large or small.
They only live in story books
And they're just not real at all,

And I know it's Willy Waters
Wrapped up in his silly sheet –
But why does he make my hair stand up
And my heart to skip a beat?

I won't go home by the churchyard.
I know I'm sure to see
Wicked Willy Waters
Waiting there for me.

ROCCO

I am St Roche's dog. We stand
Together on the painted wall:
His hat tricked with a cockleshell,
Wallet and staff in pilgrim hand.
He lifts a torn robe to display
The plague-spot. I sit up and wait.
A lot of us has peeled away.
My breed is indeterminate.
Bow! Wow!

Under a Piacenza sun
The sickness struck him like a flame.
'Dear Lord,' he cried, 'my life is done!'
And to a summer forest came.
But I, his creature, sought him high
And sought him low on his green bed
Where he had lain him down to die.
I licked his wounds and brought him bread.
Bow! Wow!

The fourteenth-century St Roche, born in Montpellier, was the patron saint of
those suffering from the plague. He spent a great part of his life on pilgrimages.
While ministering to the sick in Italy, he himself caught the plague in the town
of Piacenza. Desperately ill, he retired to the woods to die. A story tells that
here he was discovered by a dog who licked his wounds and each day brought

And he was healed, and to his house
Sick by the hundred seethed and swarmed
As, by God's grace, the Saint performed
Cures that were quite miraculous.
Now my good master's home is where
Are heavenly joys, which some declare
No fish nor bird nor beast may share.
Ask: Do I find this hard to bear?
      Bow! Wow!

him a fresh loaf of bread. In early paintings, St Roche is usually shown wearing
a cockleshell (the badge of the pilgrim) in his hat, and is accompanied by his
faithful dog. In the church of St Thomas-the-Apostle (where I was christened)
at Launceston in Cornwall is a faded medieval wall-painting of St Roche and
his dog.

DREAM POEM

I have not seen this house before
Yet room for room I know it well:
A thudding clock upon the stair,
A mirror slanted on the wall.

A round-pane giving on the park.
Above the hearth a painted scene
Of winter huntsmen and the pack.
A table set with fruit and wine.

Here is a childhood book, long lost.
I turn its wasted pages through:
Every word I read shut fast
In a far tongue I do not know.

Out of a thinness in the air
I hear the turning of a key
And once again I turn to see
The one who will be standing there.

INDEX OF FIRST LINES